THE BEACH BANK

Your TREASURE Teller

THE BEACH BANK
Your TREASURE Teller

© Copyright 1996

Kevin V. Reilly

All rights reserved. No part of this book may be reproduced in any form or by any means, electronic or mechanical, including photocopying, recording or by any information storage or retrieval system, without permission in writing from the publisher. Except in the case of brief quotations used in reviews or articles.

First Printing November 1996

Pirate Express Publishing
P. O. Box 2975
Pompano Beach, Florida 33072

ISBN 1 - 881777 - 04 - 9

Special thanks to:

Gary T. Rowe for cover design

Photo credits for the photos supplied in the book:

*Richard Rudy, Nick Schooley, Bill Babb,
Harold and Eddie Mathews, Andy Harmody,
Mark Snyder, Frank Meade, Mark Supnick.*

Thanks to all the treasure hunters who came into the shop with treasure stories, tips and suggestions for the Beach Bank book.

And thanks to my family for the support of this book.

TABLE OF CONTENTS

Beaches Along Florida's East Coast 1
Tools For Beach Digging 21
Coins & Jewelry Cleaning 27
Is It Real Or Is It Fake? 33
Dry Sand Beach Hunting Tips 41
Wet Sand Beach Hunting 45
Shallow Water Treasure Hunting! 51
Bibliography 57

INTRODUCTION

Have you ever lost anything in the sand while visiting a beach? The sand seems to gobble up whatever is dropped into it. If you a really lucky, you can pick it out of the sand in one grab. Most of the time it's lost forever. Until one day a metal detectorist walks by and gets a beep with his metal detector over that spot and scoops it up!

People have dropped gold, silver, jewelry, watches, coins and other items into the sand over the years. Even when the Spanish were shipwrecked along the coast line, they buried their treasures in the sand. Pirates, buccaneers and other drifters of the sea buried their treasures in the sand too, waiting to come back to it to recover it some day. Many people will keep depositing their lost items into the Beach Bank everyday from now on. The Beach Bank is like a savings account for the treasure hunter. People deposit their coins, valuables and other treasures into the sand and the treasure hunters have fun of making the withdrawals from the Beach Bank.

Anytime of the day when you are at the beach, you can find something while swinging your metal detector. It is an everlasting source of coins, rings, watches, chains, medallions and other items. The more populated the beaches are, the more deposits people are leaving behind in the sand for the treasure hunters.

If you happen to go to a beach without your metal detector, be a people watcher. Watch the people's reactions when they flip something off their towels. People go into a panic, look and run their hands through the sand trying to scoop up their lost items. People really don't mind if they happen to drop a few coins into the sand. On the other hand if they lost the car keys, house keys or their jewelry, this will put most people into a panic stage.

Some people deposit their lost coins and jewelry into the sand without even noticing it. When they arrive home, they realize they must have lost their items at the beach.

All in all, treasures are dropped in the sand day in and day out. If you enjoy going to the beach and swinging your metal detector, there are plenty of targets for you to recover from any beach. The softer the sand the quicker it swallows up a dropped item. If you are persistent you can find thousands of dollars in coins and jewelry and at the same time have some fun digging up all these treasures.

Remember, when you metal detect on the beach always pick up the trash you dig up and to cover your holes. This way it will keep beach hunting open for everyone. Good luck and have fun!

BEACHES ALONG FLORIDA'S EAST COAST

Along the East coast of Florida you can find your share of coins, jewelry and Spanish treasure on any given beach. Some beach sites are very well known for the Spanish treasures it can provide to the treasure hunter. Spanish treasure is found more heavily from the beaches north of the Sebastian Inlet to the south side of Ft. Pierce Inlet, about three miles down the beach. This area is also known as the Treasure Coast due to the Spanish Treasure Fleet that wrecked along the coastline in 1715. Also along these beach sections are other various shipwrecks from different time periods in history.

The 1715 treasure coins are scattered up and down the coast line. Here are some of the more popular beaches to go, and hunt for treasure coins. Bonsteel Park Beach Access, otherwise known as Chuck's Steak House beach which is about five miles north of Sebastian Inlet. Chuck's Steak House is closed, but the beach got its nick name from the restaurant being there for several years. You would want to metal detect to the north of the Bonstall Park Beach Access. Coins that are found on this beach site are usually quarters, halves and one reales. They may be tiny, but they are still Spanish treasure coins.

Bonsteel Park entrance to treasure beach.

Another very popular beach site is the Cabin Wreck site which is located at the Ambersand Beach Access parking area. This parking lot is about 2.9 miles south of Sebastian Inlet. Once on the beach you can walk about 1200 yards to the north of the walkover to the cabin. The shipwreck lies due east of the cabin. Coins are found up and down this beach during storms. The Cabin wreck got its name from Kip Wagner. Kip's cabin was the cottage for the base of his salvage operation. Kip had a name for this section of the beach he called it his Money Beach. Even today it is still producing lots of cob coins. It's still considered as the money beach today.

Wabasso Beach is another interesting beach site that produces Spanish coins. The Wabasso Beach is located at the end of C.R. 510 and the ocean. Metal detecting on this beach can produce coins dating from 1618, 1715, 1810 to present day. Keep everything you dig up along any of these beaches. You never know what may be hiding in a clump of an encrusted piece.

Frank Meade's 8 Escudo Gold Coin.

Vero Beach has a beach site known as Corrigan's for its shipwrecked coins that are washed up on its sandy beaches. This site is located between Seagrape Beach Access and Turtle Trail Beach Access. Seagrape Beach Access is located about 1.5 miles south of Wabasso Beach and Turtle Trail Beach Access is another .7 miles south of Seagrape Beach Access. Back in 1984 during Thanksgiving many coins were found on the beaches during the winter storm. Here at Corrigan's a good friend, Frank Meade, found a beautiful eight escudo gold coin. He found the gold coin by digging up an old pair of rusty pliers first. Then rechecking his hole with his metal detector, he signaled another target and while scooping again he recovered this perfectly minted gold Spanish treasure coin. What a beautiful find! Boy, was Frank really surprised with his gold coin find. Luckily he was using a pulse metal detector and had to dig all metal objects!

The Colored Beach Wreck site is located in Ft. Pierce. This beach is approximately 2.7 miles south of the Ft. Pierce Inlet. This beach is well known to most treasure hunters for finding Spanish treasure coins, both gold and silver and an occasional green uncut emerald or two. It is also known as the Nieves wreck. The Christmas tree is the center beach mark for the treasure salvagers to refer to while searching for lost treasures in the ocean. Many coins are found at this beach location.

"Mr. Gold" in front of the Christmas tree at Ft. Pierce.

When searching on the beaches for Spanish treasure, always save everything you find. It may look like trash being cover by barnacles and oxidation, but it may be something valuable. One story of a treasure hunter searching along the beach at Ft. Pierce several years ago stumbled onto some rusty old metal someone dug up previously. After seeing this object on the beach for several days he decided to bring it home with him. By his surprise, he found that this rusty old pile of junk had some hidden fortune in it. After breaking the conglomerate apart he found old iron spikes and about 10 silver eight reale cob coins. Not a bad days find for bringing home trash.

During the same Thanksgiving day storm in 1984, an old time treasure hunter recovered a large amount of Spanish treasures from the sand. Some of his treasure consisted of a few gold escudos, several silver cob coins, a piece of gold chain and many other silver and gold pieces and artifacts.

Stories have it that many years ago some of the people who walked the beaches after the storms were unfamiliar to these odd ball shaped treasure coins. That they would pick them up out of the sand and skip the coins back into the ocean. One man really had fun with them, he thought they made really good skips. Always keep your eyes on the ground for these great skipping stones, but keep them in your pocket.

During the latter part of 1994 after a few good storms, Chuck Steak House beach yielded about 800 to 900 small Spanish cob coins. The local treasure hunters found the majority of these cob coins on the beach here. These coins were found in late November.

Some of Harold's and Ed's Spanish coins found in 1994.

Several years ago at the Chuck's Steak House location there were over 2,000 Spanish coins found in a three day period after a good winter storm that hit the Florida coast.

Here is a beginners luck story, a beginner treasure hunter's first time out, went up to Corrigan's beach and found his first Spanish cob coin. That' only after buying his first metal detector and using it for the first time.

In the beginning of 1996, a friend called Lucky, went to Corrigan's beach during a storm with a few club members. With the wind blowing, the constant rain showers coming in off the ocean, all three of these treasure hunters kept on detecting the wet sand beach. This is also the first time Lucky metal detected on the Treasure Coast beaches during a storm. Lucky, of course, got lucky, he found three small Spanish coins on the beach after a few hours of being there. Lucky was astounded with his treasure coins he found. The other two club members also found treasure coins too.

Waves cutting into the dunes on one of the treasure beaches.

Somewhere along the beach between Ft. Pierce Inlet and the Colored Beach site, Spanish silver Portrait Dollars are found on the beach after a good storm.

While metal detecting on Ft. Pierce beach always keep your eyes open for unusual objects. Someone had found some green colored rocks on the beach here. These small rocks turned out to be uncut emeralds. Keep your eyes on the ground while searching, you may find an emerald someday, too!

If you happen to find a small cob coin or two, keep them in a safe place until you get back to your car. A friend one day years back took the half reale out of his pocket to show his hunting buddy the coin. Before the hunting buddy could take a look at the coin, a strong gust of wind blew the coin out of his hand. It took him three extra hours searching for this one single coin that blew out of his palm of his hand with the wind. He did finally find the coin hours later.

Jensen Beach, which is located south of Ft. Pierce, is a beach that may produce a Spanish coin or two. This beach is more popular for its everyday lost coins and jewelry.

The beach in Stuart is also good to metal detect for lost coins & jewelry.

Dubois Park located on the south side of Jupiter inlet is a good family beach and is excellent to metal detect. On this beach here you'll never know what you will dig up. Most of the time it will be common everyday coins and jewelry. It can also be a Spanish silver or gold coin from the shipwreck that is settled in the ocean just a couple hundred yards off the beach. The Spanish coins sometimes get uncovered after a good size storm or a couple of days of Northeast wind.

In 1995 they were adding sand to the beach in Jupiter to make the beach wider for the beach restoration project. When the state does a major beach restoration project like that it brings out all types of treasure hunters. These treasure hunters are looking for coins, jewelry, Spanish treasure and even Mother Nature's treasures which are shells. Shell collectors really have more fun seeking out their treasure after a project like this.

Also in Dubois Park is a little swimming area that is roped off for children & parents to swim in. This area is located on the inside of the inlet on the southern bank. There is also a tide pond families wade in, in the summertime. Both of these areas are great for shallow water hunters. They can produce some nice gold jewelry pieces from time to time. You can definitely find your share of coins here. One summer day a woman was sitting in her beach chair in the tide pond digging her hands into the sands bottom. She uncovered a round object, which turned out to be an 1800 dollar size silver coin. So, you never know what you can find.

Just on the north side of the Jupiter Inlet is the Jupiter Lighthouse. There is plenty of history in this area for all the history buffs. A couple of Seminole War's were fought in this area back in the 1800's.

Carlin Park, a good family beach park for both children and adults. This is a good area to metal detect both in the shallow water when the ocean is calm and on the beach looking for lost jewelry and coins. It is possible to dig an old shipwreck coin out of the sand here on the right day.

During winter storms Juno Beach can produce a good quantity of old American silver coins, clad coins and jewelry. Every once in a while you may turn up an old small piece of a treasure coin here too.

Along the beaches in West Palm Beach there are few public beach accesses and the parking meters are expensive. If you can find your way to these beaches along this area and get up behind some of the exclusive hotels, you'll be surprised at what you may find. Good luck. Since West Palm Beach is an older area of Florida, silver coins are found here regularly during winter storms or after a hurricane. It's always fun to dig up a few turn of the century American silver coins. Finding gold jewelry on any of the beaches in West Palm Beach can be very exciting.

Lake Worth Beach is a very popular beach that has a fishing pier. Both the dry sand beach and shallow water can produce some nice jewelry and coins. Go where the crowd is sunbathing on the beach and you should do well. A friend while snorkeling with his metal detector one day last summer stumbled into eight $20.00 bills drifting along the bottom near the sand.

The shallow water around the Lake Worth pier yields some excellent finds. Somedays the water gives up several gold rings to the shallow water treasure hunters. One day last summer, some local shallow water treasure hunters found 38 gold rings among them. When the ocean is right, it will produce good quantities of gold jewelry and coins.

Just recently a treasure hunter metal detecting in the dry sand by Lake Worth's pier found a beautiful three ounce, 22K gold bracelet. The unique part of this bracelet was the ornate charms that was attached to it. What a great find that came out of the dry sand.

Boynton Beach, the public beach in the area is a good beach to metal detect both in the surf and on the sand. A person can find lots of lost coins and jewelry on the beach here.

Delray Beach is located at the end of east Atlantic Ave. This beachfront had the beach restored to it a few years back making the beach wider for the beach go'ers to loose more items. This is an excellent beach to metal detect. The beach is located across from some local stores and restaurants that bring in all types of people. Keep yours eyes open to see where all the beach go'ers are laying on the sand and metal detect those areas later on in the evening. This beach has produced some very nice jewelry pieces that have been found in the dry sand.

Somewhere on the southern end of Delray Beach, Spanish silver cob coins turn up occasionally after a good northeaster. Some of these coins are in pretty nice shape and condition. The Spanish coins that have been found here were both eight and four reales. Several were found over the years including a small silver bar about the size of a folding pocket knife.

Driving south on A1A the next public area for great beach hunting is Boca Raton. Boca has many miles of beach front. There are plenty of parking areas to park at to get to the beaches. There is also allot of history in Boca Raton.

Spanish River Boulevard is the most northern beach area in Boca Raton. There are some parking places along the street at Spanish River Blvd. There is a park called Spanish River Park right there close to the street that has ample parking areas in it. On this section of the beach you can find just about anything. You mostly find clad coins and pennies with an occasional piece of jewelry. Back in 1984 this beach yielded over $45.00 in old silver American coins, with two people metal detecting, in just a 3 day period during a storm. This beach in the past has turned up Spanish silver coins. You just have to get lucky metal detecting around this beach.

Just north a few hundred yards of Spanish River Park Beach there is a story that pirates came ashore onto this beach hundreds of years ago for fresh water. A fresh water spring is somewhere in this area. Doing a little research of the area can yield some interesting old finds.

Red Reef Park is another beach in Boca. When detecting this beach, keep everything you find. You may turn up a small silver cob coin from one of the old shipwrecks. A couple of beach hunters found some old small Spanish coins here a few years back after a northeaster. This area of the beach is also good for finding the old American silver coins from the turn of the century.

Back in the 1920's while the road crew was building the new A1A, a pouch of Spanish silver cob coins were unearthed. These coins were eight reales.

At the end of Palmetto Park Blvd. is another beach worth exploring. This beach is small and sometimes rocky. Coins and other items can get wedge into the rocky areas making it hard to scoop up targets.

You may want to bring a narrow trowel or screw driver to this beach with you. This is an excellent beach for coins and gold jewelry. A beautiful one carat diamond ring was found on the beach in the dry sand this year.

Just about a quarter mile south of Palmetto Park Blvd. on the beachside, a few years ago after a storm, a ten foot cannon became exposed. This cannon has been buried under the sand right at the dune line. If you can imagine, the cannon was pointing out towards the ocean like it was ready to fire at the enemy. After the storm past, the sand filled the beach back in and the cannon disappeared again under the sand until the next big storm.

For the divers, around Boca Raton inlet on the ocean side, many ships have gone to the bottom resting in the sands. Exploring these areas off to the east of the inlet you may find a piece of treasure from one of the many ships that have sunk in past times. Story has it that there is a Spanish Galleon under the sand just off the inlet somewhere. You have to get really lucky to find it and do allot of research to figure out where the general area is located.

At one time hundreds of years ago, story has it that Boca Raton had three inlets for the sailors to enter. Two of these three inlets were natural and would fill in from time to time. One of these inlets may be located on the northern end of the beach. The inlet in Boca Raton today is said to be located about one mile south of the old inlet from years past. You may want to research these inlet areas more closer to see where they may have been. They could turn up some interesting artifacts and history.

Just south of the Boca Raton Inlet is South Inlet Park. This is the only real beach access to this beach area. The parking fee into the park is quite expensive, unless you are a resident of Boca Raton. This section of beach is very interesting to metal detect. Back in the 1920's Boca Raton had some large old hotels on this beach to cater to the wealthy people. Coins can be found here dating anywhere from the late 1800's all the way to present day. Some nice antique pieces of jewelry were recovered from this beach. Back many years ago, we metal detected along this beach front. We found all types of silver coins dating from 1902 to the early 1945 scattered all around the beach. Being so close to the inlet, Spanish cob coins are found here a few times during the year. You have to be patient metal detecting this beach area, because you never know what you find next.

Back in the early 1980's an iron cannon was resting in the sand on the inside of the southern side of the inlet. It sat there for years until one day it disappeared. Either someone decided to take it for their collection or it got buried up from the shifting sand again.

The next town south of Boca Raton is Deerfield Beach in Broward County. Every year, Deerfield Beach is announced, being one of the nicest and cleanest beaches in Broward County. Close to the street the beach area has green grass and benches so people can sit on them. The beach itself is normally clean of all unwanted trash. The sand is soft for people to loose things. Metal detecting along this sandy beach produces many lost coins and jewelry. Quite a number of gold and silver jewelry has been found both on the beach and in the surf. There are reports that there are a couple of Rolex watches lost in the water. If you shallow water hunt you may come across one of these watches one day. Another ring that was reported lost in the water is a 2 carat diamond ring and it is still waiting for some lucky water hunter to recover it!

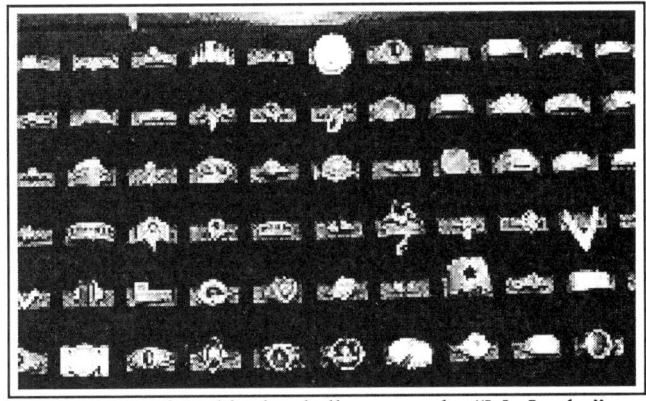

Gold rings found in the shallow water by "Mr. Lucky".

Deerfield Beach also has a public pier. It is located one block north of the Hillsboro Blvd. The south side of the pier is where most activity is happening. Metal detecting here can be a treat. Deerfield Beach also has small rock jetties every couple of hundred feet or so, the entire length of its beach. These jetties help keep the beach from eroding away. The jetties also help collect coins and jewelry next to the rocks. While searching around the rocks be careful not to damage your coil on the rocks. You may want to have a small trowel in your back pocket to get to some of the targets lost close to the rocks. Also, a smaller coil can help to get in and around the rocks easier. Keep your eyes open for sand to wash out along the jetties. You can recover lots of treasure in the small areas around the rocks.

Looking south from Deerfield Beach's fishing pier.

On the south side of Deerfield Beach, the beach seems more isolated. It is a little tougher to metal detect this area. Be patient, because the treasure may surprise you. One day an old time treasure hunter would venture to the south end of the beach just to get away from the crowds of people on the north end of the beach. While metal detecting he recovered a beautiful 2 1/2 carat diamond cocktail ring, set in 18K gold. What a find and what an exciting feeling it brings when he found out the diamond was real.

Traveling further south down A1A, you pass over another bridge which is the Hillsboro Inlet. This inlet has allot of history in the

Pompano Beach area.

In the vicinity of Hillsboro Inlet there are many stories of shipwrecks on the Hillsboro Rocks. On the south side of the inlet Spanish coins are found occasionally in the sand. These coins are dredged up out of the inlet while the dredge operator is removing sand from clogging the inlet. Keep a good look-out on the dredge operation for best timing to find these Spanish coins. While the dredge is being operated, this will be the best time to be at the site to see what is spewing out of the dredge's pipe. Be very careful not to get too close to the sand that is being pumped out of the dredge. Working around the dredge tailings can be profitable. Some of the coins found that are dredged up are Spanish silver coins. A 1715 piece of eight came up recently from the dredge. You will find quite of bit of modern coinage and an occasional piece of jewelry too. A few years back, the dredge threw out over 22 Spanish cob coins. These coins were all shapes and sizes.

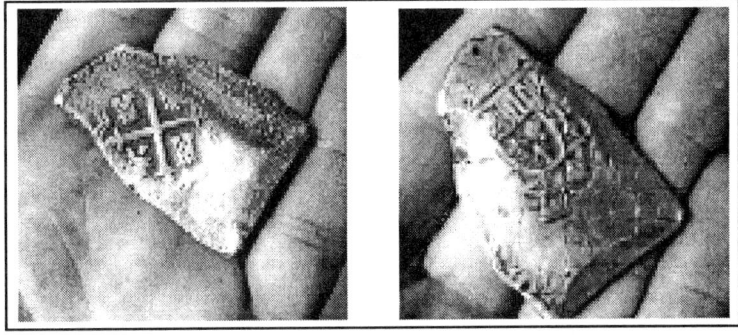

Front and back of piece of eight found at Hillsboro Inlet.

At the end of East Atlantic Blvd. is a parking are for Pompano Beach, just to the north of this parking lot is Pompano's Municipal pier. There is a huge parking lot there and there are parking meters along the street. This is a very popular beach for both the shallow water hunter and the beach hunter. On calm days it is nice to get in the water for some shallow water hunting. The south side of the pier seems to be much more productive in both coins and jewelry than it is on the north side of the pier. In the dry sand, there are many different areas to metal detect. There is also a playground area for children on the beach. It is an excellent area for people to loose coins and jewelry while watching their children on the swings. A few years back a nice one carat diamond ring with emeralds surrounding the diamond came out from under the swing set.

Pompano Beach looking north to the pier.

A shallow water treasure hunter was in the water metal detecting for a few hours and came up with 26 pieces of gold. There were 4 gold rings and 22 gold charms found that day along with a few dollars in change. Another time a water hunter found a Rolex watch in the water here. Even something strange came out of the water in Pompano, someone found a whole roll of quarters in the water with one scoop of his water scoop.

There is a story of a girl who lost a 5 foot long gold chain in the shallow water one year. She said the chain was 14K and she wore it around her waist. She was very upset when she told one of the local treasure hunters about losing it. Good luck, maybe you can find this lost chain if the ocean and the sand cooperates someday.

On both sides of the fishing pier in Pompano Beach, occasionally silver Spanish coins gets washed ashore here. During the beach restoration project in 1982, a 5" piece of gold chain & an 8 Escudo gold coin were recovered by one lucky shell collector. Pompano Beach is also well known for its popularity for the beach-go'ers. Many lost modern coins & jewelry are found on this beach.

Each year in the spring Pompano has its famous Seafood Festival on the beach. The city closes down the beach road and a short span of Atlantic Blvd. for a weekend festival. After the festival has ended on Sunday, the next morning the beach is loaded with metal detectorists. They find many lost coins, jewelry and paper money from the leftovers of the festival. You can really clean up in money for a few days after the festival. One of the local treasure hunters found $87.00 in paper money and coins the evening after the fair.

There were two silver bars found at the Hillsboro Rocks by an old man many years ago, around the turn of the century, believed to have come from an old Spanish Galleons that wrecked. Story has it the man who found these bars thought they were lead and were using the bars for door stops. It was later on when he found out these two bars were made of silver.

One friend came up with a jar and it was full of pennies while he was water hunting one afternoon. What a surprise look on his face when he dug this out of the water.

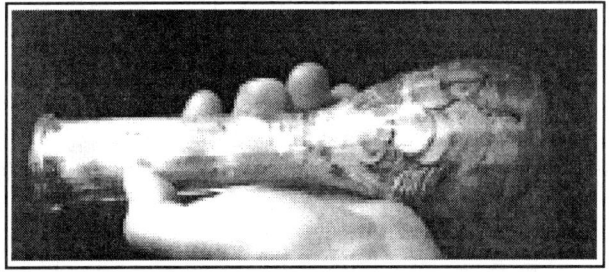

Jar of pennies found while out water hunting.

Lauderdale-By-The-Sea produces lots of coins and jewelry over the years. About a mile north of the Commercial Blvd. pier Spanish shipwreck coins have been found by local metal detectorists after strong storms. Many old ships have been destroyed by storms. One can never tell when the next piece of eight will turn up on this section of the beach. The beach area by the fishing pier in Lauderdale-By-The-Sea produces thousands of lost coins each month for the treasure hunter. The beach is very popular due to all the stores and restaurants here by the beach. This section of beach brings a lots of tourists to the beach every year. Shallow water hunting is excellent here. It seems that most of the lost items are on the north side of the fishing pier.

The coastline along Fort Lauderdale beach can be a very productive beach to explore. This area of beach front has produced thousands of pieces of lost jewelry and millions of coins for the beach hunters. Along this beach a person can find old shipwreck coins from the Spain, England and other countries of the world. After a good strong wind and strong waves these beaches produce a number of old silver American coins. These old coins can be found anywhere along the beach from the north end of the strip area all the way down to the southern end of the beach and even down to the inlet. Ft. Lauderdale beach attracts all kinds of tourists from all over the world and is very popular for the metal detectorist. Besides finding coins and jewelry, coins from all over the world are found here. You never know what you'll dig up in the sand next at the beach. One day last year a man's Rolex divers watch came out of the dry sand. A 3 carat diamond ring was found in the dry sand next to a picnic table on the beach.

Fort Lauderdale Beach looking north.

The beach just south of Port Everglades Inlet is John Lloyd State Park. Unfortunately this beach is off limits to metal detecting. Every once in a while someone gets permission to metal detect along the wet sand of the beach. It depends on which park ranger you talk to at the entrance of the park, before you drive into the park. Really, the only area that the park rangers sometimes let you detect is between the waters edge and the high tide line. Good luck on getting permission.

Dania & Hollywood beaches are very productive for finding lost coins & jewelry. In the winter these beaches become very busy with the tourists from the north and Canada. Anywhere along any of these beaches you can find coins, silver jewelry, gold jewelry and watches. Hollywood has a large area of beach, you may want to check out the beaches and see where most of the people sunbathe and gather at. This will determine where you will want to metal detect for the most producing treasures.

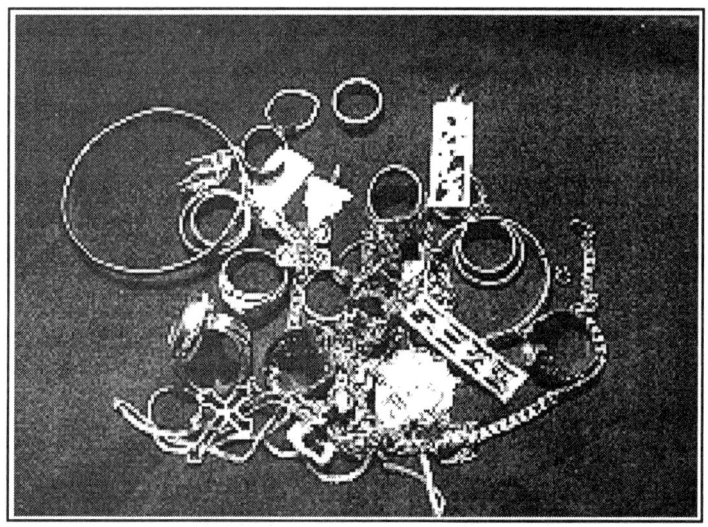

Gold rings and other gold jewelry found in the ocean.

In Hollywood one day, one of the local treasure hunters found 14 gold rings and 8 silver rings in an afternoon. He also recovered about $ 20.00 in change. A heavy link 14K gold bracelet was found in the dry sand a few months ago. Also, a 14K gold chain with 4 gold charms and a ring on it came out of the dry sand back in 1991. The total weight of the chain, charms and ring weighed over 3 ounces.

Hallandale Beach is another good beach to metal detect. Coins, rings and watches are found in the sand here. A few years back a half dozen or so silver cob coins were recovered by a treasure hunter during a strong, windy storm.

Going further south on A1A Haulover Beach is a fine beach to go metal detecting. There is also a fishing pier at this beach. A number of items usually gets lost around piers. A pier at any beach attracts people, for fishing, sight-seeing and visiting.

Driving further south along the scenic road of A1A is Miami Beach. There are public beach accesses to get on the beach in some of the areas between all the hotels & high risers that are scattered along the coastline here. Anywhere between 80th. Street and 5th. Street on Miami Beach can be very productive in coins and jewelry. Miami Beach is good to metal detect in the daylight hours. Since Miami Beach has been used for many decades, it has accumulated millions of coins & jewelry over the years. When there are storms, the sand does shift and opens up money pockets up and down the beaches here. Hundreds of coins can be recovered in a money pocket. If you stumble into a money pocket, be patient, you may find that you will be in the jewelry pocket too. Good luck, maybe one day you will find one of these money pockets on the next trip to the beaches here in Miami.

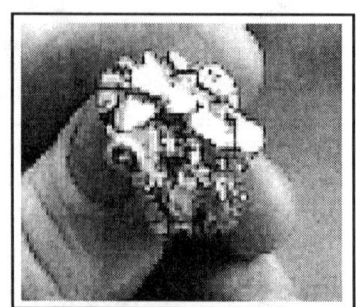

14k gold nugget ring weighs over 1 ounce.

Located along the Rickenbacker Causeway, going towards Key Biscayne, is a beach area known to the locals as Hobie Beach, Sailboard Beach or windsurf beach and also jet ski beach. This is an area where people launch their Hobie Cats, windsurfers or jet skies at. Its a protected area from the oceans waves. It is also a great area for the shallow water treasure hunters to venture out into the bay looking for lost coins, jewelry and watches. For years this area packs out with people in the summer with swimmers and water people. Before the crowds get there or after they leave is an opportune time to metal detect the shallow waters. If you venture into the water here, there are some rules to remember. You can dig in the sand, but you cannot dig in the Turtle Grass. Digging in Turtle Grass is off limits and you could probably get into some trouble digging there. Digging in the sand is great, especially when you are recovering coins & lost jewelry.

Gold coin from necklace found in the shallow waters.

As you drive east out towards Key Biscayne, Crandon Park, is located on the left hand side of the road. This is an excellent park to shallow water treasure hunt at. This beach-park is packed on weekends with all the locals from Miami that come to relax and have fun at the beach. Since this is a protected beach front from the oceans waves it is calm most of the time here. Occasionally this beach gets some rough waters with waves in the bay, but most of the time it is calm. Metal detecting here is tedious, mainly because of the full time treasure hunters who come here all the time. If you have patience, the pickings are slim, but this place is loaded with gold jewelry and few coins. A scarce area for metal detecting, but there is allot of gold jewelry found here. One of the full time water hunters found 11 gold rings here one day metal detecting in an afternoon. Patience pays, so good luck.

At the end of Key Biscayne is a state park called Cape Florida. You cannot metal detect in the park or on the sand, but you can metal detect in the shallow water. It is also a good area to find lost coins & jewelry. You may find a cob coin here too. This park is filled with history. Ask the park rangers for the history of the park. You may dig up some old shipwrecked coin or a piece of an old ship. Try a little shallow water hunting out here, you may find a nice gold ring or two and definitely plenty of coins.

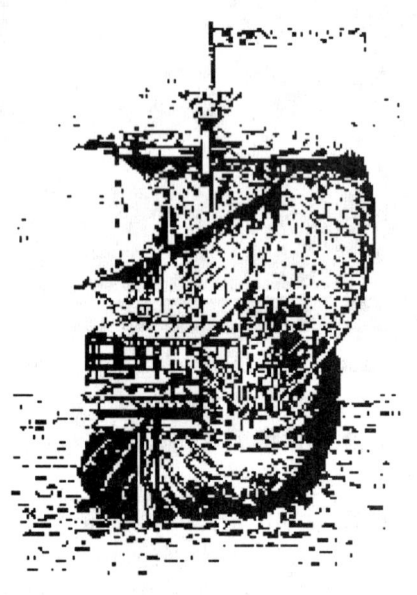

TOOLS FOR BEACH DIGGING

While you are ready to head towards your favorite beach, you are going to need something to dig in the sand with. There are all types of digging tools available for digging in sand. Beach hunters use different types of sand scoops and some beach hunters get out their shovels. In this section of the book, we will take a look at some of the different items needed to dig in the sand and also in the water. In some shallow water areas you may also need a floating sifter to throw your targets into to retrieve your treasures.

The basic of all scoops for the sand is the sand scoop. There are a few manufacturers that have different names for the scoops, but the scoops all do the same thing, sift sand. The sand scoop is a hand held scoop with either wire mesh screening on it or holes punched out in the bucket. The hand sand scoop is a sifting device that will allow you to bend over and dig into the sand to retrieve your targets. Sifting with a screen on the scoop will sift the sand out quickly. The scoops with the holes punched into the body will need a couple of extra shakes to get the sand out. The hand scoops with screening on them will work out better down along the wet sand. The scoops with the holes in them tend to get clogged with the wet sand and don't sift the sand out that well. If you only have a scoop with holes in it and you are in the wet sand, you'll have to scoop and dump out the sand. You can really shake the scoop harder to get the sand out if this is all you have to work with. Remember in the wet sand the screen scoops are much easier and faster to sift. A galvanized steel hand sand scoop should last you three to five years before rusting.

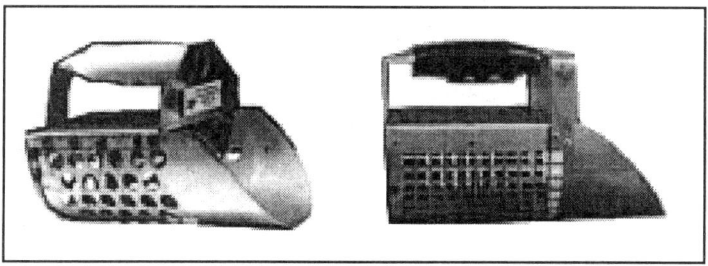

Two different styles of sand scoops.

The next most common sand scoop that you may see people using is a long handle scoop. These scoops help to recover your target more quickly, because you don't have to bend down all the time. The long handle scoop also helps save your back if you have any back trouble. There are all shapes and sizes of long handled scoops out on the market today. All of these scoops will sift sand. The size and length of the handles are up to you. You have to make the choice yourself for which scoop you want to use. Some of these long handled scoops have break apart handles that are great for traveling. Again, the scoops with screen will sift faster than the one with the holes in it. If you only dig in the dry sand, you can use either the screen scoops or the scoops with holes in it. Both these two style scoops will work fine.

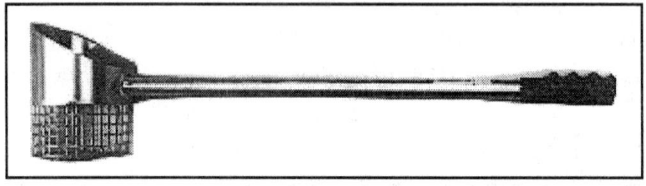

A long handled scoop makes it easy to recover your treasures!

The scoops you may see next out on the beach are used in the wet sand and sometimes in the water. These scoops are made with heavy wire screen mesh to sift the wet sand fast. These scoops usually have a longer handle on it about 40" long. In some cases these scoops are reinforced with all kinds of brackets and braces so you can step on the back and push the scoop in with your foot. The scoops can also be used in shallow water hunting as long as you don't get into a rocky area. Rocks and shells can collapse the screening on the scoops if digging in this type of ground condition. The screened scoops work very well in wet sandy areas.

For the person who will be shallow water hunting, there are several different style water scoops available. You would want a good, strong water scoop that is very dependable for water hunting. Imagine, getting out into the water with all your gear and not having the right water scoop to retrieve your targets. This is very frustrating. Or you have a scoop you built yourself and not realizing it, after ten or fifteen minutes into the hunt the handle breaks off right at the connection of the bucket of your scoop. This can ruin a day for most people.

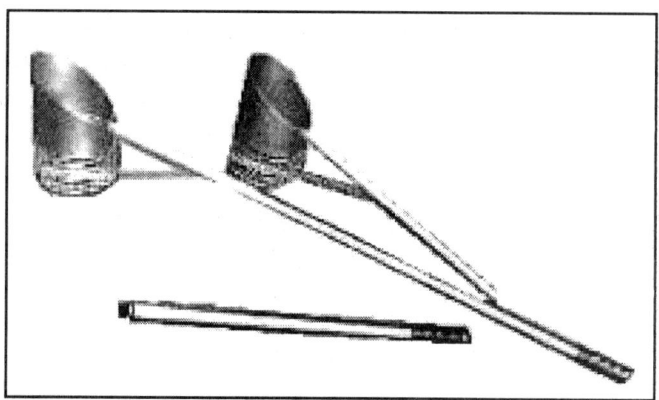

The Beachmaster Water Scoop and The Travel Scoop above.

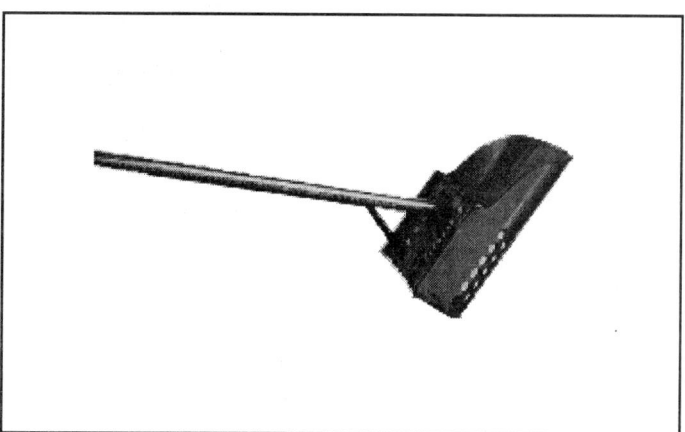

Pictured above is an all stainless steel water scoop.

What you would like in a shallow water scoop is durability. The bucket should be at least 16 gauge metal. The scoop buckets can be made of either steel, stainless steel or aluminum. It should have holes punched through-out the bucket for sifting the sand. This water scoop should have a long handle on it minimum of forty inches or so. The handle can be made of galvanized steel, stainless steel, aluminum or wood.

Wood handles usually deteriorate in salt ocean water faster and then snap in half. Galvanized handles will last longer, but the galvanized handle will pit and rust in time. Stainless steel handles on water scoops should last for a long, long time. The stainless handles will not rust at all. Stainless steel is much more expensive in price than just a steel scoop. The water scoops are usually reinforced in places. These scoops may even have a foot pad mounted on the back of the scoop to kick the scoop into the sand. Some water scoops are designed to use the back of the scoop for your foot pad. The water scoops are made not to crush. The scoops usually have holes punched through-out the scoop's bucket. Having holes in the bucket will keep the bucket from crushing if you are hunting in rocky or shelly areas. These scoops are usually designed for rugged digging in the water.

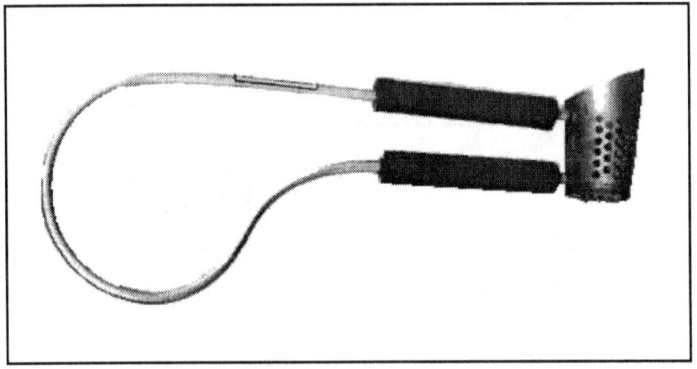

This scoop has an aluminum handle, stainless steel bucket & foam floats.

The stainless steel scoops will not rust in salt water. The plain steel scoops will rust right away in the salt water. A steel scoop is fine to use, all you need to do is wash it off every time and spray it with WD-40 or some other type of oil, still it will rust. The galvanized steel on handles in salt water will last a year or so, depending on how you take care and rinse the scoop off with fresh water.   An all stainless steel water scoop should last you a long time. Depending on how rough you are with your equipment, really depends on how long the equipment will last you.

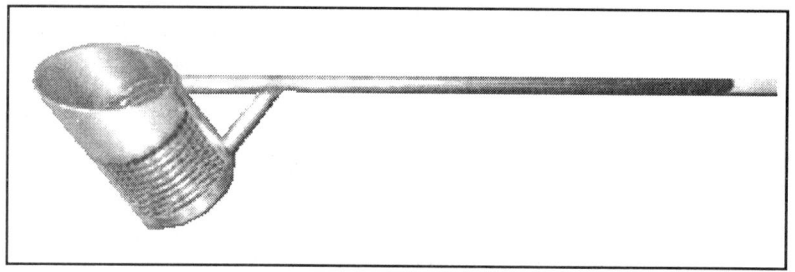

This 6" diameter water scoop has screening on it for quick sifting.

A short handled scoop.

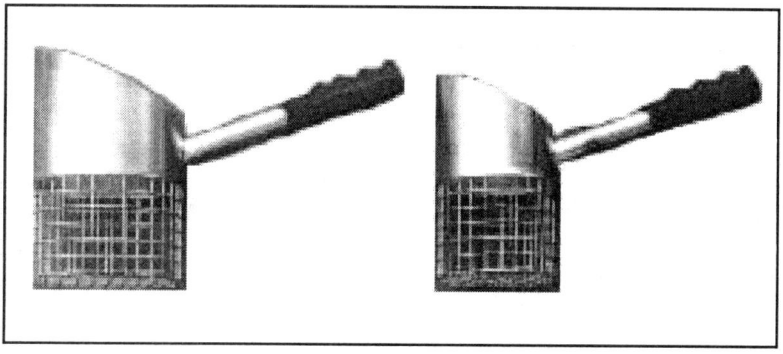

A couple of other style sand scoops for the beach.

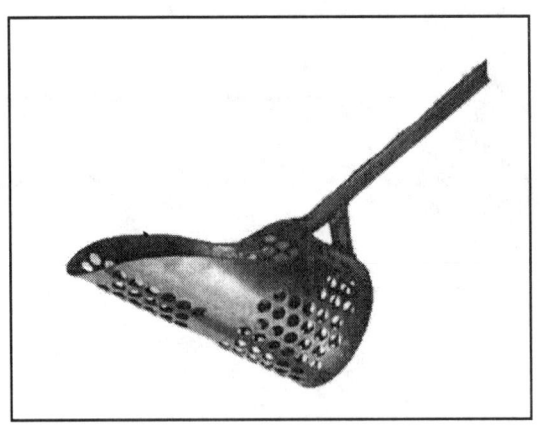

The all stainless steel monster scoop for deep digging.

If you are in a rocky or shelly area in the water, you may want to tote along a floating sifting device with you. These are easy to make with a few items you may have to purchase. The floating screen is made to dump your scoop bucket you just scooped out of the water to check for your finds. Since you are hunting in rocks and shells these items fill your scoop bucket up full and you cannot retrieve your treasure without pulling out all the shells from the scoop. Dumping the scoopful into the floating sifter makes it easy to spread your shells and rocks around so you can find the target faster. If you are metal detecting in the shallow water in the sand, this floating sifter is useless. Once you bring the bucket out of the water to dump it into the floating sifter, the sand is usually gone out of the bucket leaving only the treasure in the scoop's bucket.

The floating sifter can be made with a car inner tube, some wood for a frame and some half inch wire mesh screen. It can also be made easier with a Garrett Gold Classifier Pan and a 13" automobile inner tube. You should be able to purchase the inner tube at any automotive store or gas station. With the gold classifier you can substitute the inner tube with a Styrofoam ring. The styrofoam ring can be purchased at any pool store or craft store.

COINS & JEWELRY CLEANING

After you spend hours metal detecting for coins and jewelry and unearthing these treasures out of the sand, there is one common question. How do I get all these coins and jewelry that I have found cleaned? This question is asked by most people. There are several ways to clean coins and jewelry you found. In the next few chapters, there will be several suggestions. You may like one of the ideas or you may like using your own method. As long as it works for you, that's all that counts.

The biggest question is usually, how do I clean all the coins I gathered up from metal detecting. One way is to wash them, and the easiest way is with a rock tumbler. You can usually purchase a rock tumbler at a lapidary store, metal detecting store and maybe even a hobby shop. If you are a bargain hunter, you may find a rock tumbler at the flea market or even in a garage sale. You have to keep your eyes open for them.

There is a product out on the market today put out by Finch Products called the Magic Tumble Clean. This is a solution to add to your rock tumbler for cleaning the dirty coins you have found. With this solution it will take about 1 to 2 hours to clean the coins. The Magic Tumble Clean kit sells for around $15.00. The kit includes special treated tumbling media and special cleaning compound and a set of instructions. All you need is your tumbler, a little water and time.

Rock tumblers come in various sizes. They range in size from a 1-1/2 pound barrel, 3 pound barrel, 4-1/2 pound barrel, 6 pound and 12 pound barrels. The two most common sizes are the 3 and 4-1/2 pound barrels. The 3 pound barrel holds around 120 to 180 coins at one time. The 4-1/2 pound barrel will hold around 200 to 450 coins at one time. The barrel rests on a set of parallel bars and one of the bars is connected to a motor. When the tumbler is working, the barrel lays sideways on these bars and rolls over and over, hundreds of turns. When your dirty coins are in the barrel with your cleaning solution, the coins wind up tumbling over one another until they get clean. It's similar to how a washing machine cleans clothes. Anyway, it can take a few hours to clean the coins.

Coins and other items in tumbler barrel.

Here are some other cleaning solutions for the tumbler. A common cleaning solution to use is liquid dishwashing soap, a handful of beach sand, a handful of pebbles, water and the dirty coins. Using this solution will take about 3 to 5 hours to clean the coins. Make sure if you use this method, you don't dump out the coins into your kitchen sink. The easiest way to get the coins separated from the pebbles and sand is to dump out the coins and water into a sieve or a sand scoop outside. This way you don't make a huge mess in the house. Another mixture that works well in a tumble is a handful of pebbles, dishwashing soap, a table spoon of white vinegar, water and the coins. This second solution takes about 2 to 4 hours to clean the coins. If you use the vinegar mixture make sure you separate the pennies from the clad coins and nickels. If you don't, the pennies will turn your clad coins and nickels orange. When you use the solution with the sand, it may take longer but you can clean all your coins together without separating the pennies from the clad coins. In fact, when I clean my coins I use the sand solution with the pebbles, soap and water. But instead of putting just coins into the tumbler, I also put the keys, car toys, lead sinkers and other miscellaneous small junk that I may have found in the barrel too. It all comes out clean, it may take up to 5 hours to clean the items, but I'm in no rush. You may have your own tumbling solution that you use which works fine too. These are just some suggestions for you to try.

Coins being tumbled in rock tumbler.

Using the tumbler for cleaning silver coins and jewelry is best when using Finch Products, Magic Tumble Clean. This product does a very nice job to silver and gold items. You should not put any valuable collectible coins through the tumbling process. If you have a coin that is questionable, bring it to a coin expert and don't try to clean the coin yourself. Key date coins should not be cleaned in a tumbler or any other cleaning solutions. That's where the expert coin professionals come in.

Another way to clean silver coins or silver jewelry that comes out of the salt oceans shoreline is to use an electrolysis method. There are a few of these units out on the market. An electrolysis unit will usually clean one coin at a time. There are other books available in the library to give you ideas how electrolysis units actually operate. You may even be able to purchase these books in your local treasure hunting store.

Electrolysis cleaner.

Here is a fast and easy way to clean silver coins (not key date collectible coins) and silver jewelry that have no precious stones in them. This method will also clean your silverware too.

The cleaning method works on the same principle of electrolysis, but only costs a few pennies to make.

Take a small plastic bowl, one that you only want to use for this cleaning purpose all the time. Next, take some aluminum foil and put it into the bottom of the plastic bowl. Set your silver coins, silver jewelry and other silver items into the bowl on top of the aluminum. Keep all the items away from one another, meaning, don't put a coin on top of another coin. Keep them separated. (Remember, do not clean key date collectible coins with this method.) Take a table spoon and scoop out two scoops of baking soda and put it into the bowl covering the silver.

Next, boil water in a pot or kettle. Make sure the water is boiled and be careful not to get the water on you because it is so hot. Pour the boiling water into the bowl with the solution and the silver. Step away and don't breath the fumes. After the water cools down, rinse the silver items in a sink. Throw away the water and recycle the aluminum foil.

The coins will be clean and they will have a grayish tint to them. Final step is to make a paste solution in the palm of your hand with baking soda and a few drops of water. Next, rub the paste onto the silver coins or silver jewelry, rubbing the grayish tint away. Rinse with water and your items should be sparkling silver shiney. Good luck and have fun.

Here are a few other methods of coin cleaning ideas from other treasure hunters I've talked with. I haven't tried these methods yet myself, but you can, if you want to. In a rock tumbler one person uses old coffee grinds with a water and soap solution. Another treasure hunter uses cut up brillo pads in his rock tumbler along with soap and water.

Coins that were cleaned with a rock tumbler.

One other treasure hunter uses crushed walnut shells to tumble his coins. Another person puts vinegar and salt into a plastic container, separates the clad coins and nickels from the pennies and lets the coins soak in the solution for about 35 minutes.

Remember! Cleaning coins that you have dug up while metal detecting is good. But, do not clean the rare or key date collectible coins that are valuable. Cleaning these coins yourself can make the valuable coins worthless. Have a coin expert do the cleaning on these coins for you. If in doubt, let an expert take a look at the coins that are questionable. Also, for you to get an idea of which coins are valuable, buy yourself a coin pricing book at any book store. This book will teach you quite a bit about coins.

Cleaning clad coins, nickels and pennies for spending or saving is very enjoyable. It is nice to have clean coins to bring to the bank or to spend. Bankers and store owners won't frown on you with clean coins.

A pile of cleaned coins from one time in a rock tumbler.

Whatever means you have to getting your coins clean is the secret. Tumbling the coins is the easiest way of all. Good luck.

IS IT REAL OR IS IT FAKE?

You have a collection of jewelry that you found while metal detecting along the beaches in the last few months. Some of the jewelry says 14K, some other pieces say .585 and maybe some pieces say H.G.E. What does this all mean, you think. Well, first of all, the fact is, is it real gold or junk.

Here is a break down of the karats verses percentages in jewelry. Most jewelry made in the United States is usually one of three grades of gold. There is 18 karat, which is also known as .750, 14 karat, which is known as .585 and you have 10 karat gold. 10 karat gold is sometimes marked as .417, but most of the time it is stamped at 10K.

Irish gold, most of the time you'll see it at 9K or 9 Karat. In gold jewelry from around the world, the stamps inside the pieces are 98% stamped in decimals, rather than in karats.

If you have found a gold ring and it is stamped 14K P. You have nothing to worry about. The "P" next to the karat marking means that the gold ring is 14 karat plum. Meaning, it is true 14 karat or 13.5 karat true. In years past, some jewelers might have marked a ring at 14K, but really it is 11.5K or 12K in reality. With the "P" marked next to the karat, you know you have a solid 14 karat or so gold jewelry.

Some jewelry may be marked with the letters H.G.E. This marking stands for Heavy Gold Electroplate. Or in other words, commonly known as junk jewelry to the treasure hunter. G. F. or Gold Filled, is another way of saying the ring is not solid gold, but a small percentage of the ring is filled with gold. Markings stamped in the ring saying G. P., Gold Plated means the outer layer of the ring has a gold plating on it. You may find a chain saying 14K Sterling on it. This stamp means that you have found a silver chain with 14K plating over the chain to give it a gold look. A chain like this would make it look like its real gold, but it is an inexpensive piece of jewelry.

When you find gold rings and other gold jewelry here and there, you start to become more aware of the gold. When a gold ring is found, normally you can tell if it is real gold or junk just by looking at the piece and feeling the weight. Gold is a heavy metal. It does have weight to it if its in a ring or other type of jewelry piece.

Silver is another metal that has markings in it. The stamp .925 means that the item is sterling silver or 92.5% silver and 7.5% copper. American silver coins are 90% silver and 10% copper. Mexico silver can be stamped on the jewelry as .720 or Mexico. The .720 marking is 72% silver.

Platinum is a metal that is also made in jewelry. The stamp markings in platinum is either Pt. or Plat. Platinum is usually more precious than gold. Sometimes you may find a gold ring with a diamond in the ring with the diamond set in platinum.

Now, that you have found a ring or two and they have no markings in them. How can you tell if the ring you found is real gold or junk. You can bring the pieces you found into a jewelry store and pawn shop and ask them if they can test your item for you. Or you can purchase your own gold testing kit from your local treasure hunting store or jewelry supply shop. These kits contain acids which are made for testing gold and silver. The acid kits have acids for testing 10K, 14K, 18K and even a 22K gold and a testing stone. In some of the kits there may be a silver acid for testing silver. Testing gold and silver are simple and the kits come with a set of instructions to show you how.

For testing a gold item, you would rub the gold item onto the testing stone leaving a gold scratch on the stone. Next, you would take out the 10K acid and put the liquid acid over the scratched gold mark that is on the stone. If the line stays on the stone holding to the 10K acid, the item is at least 10K. Next try the 14K acid and if the line stays with the 14K acid the item is at least 14K. Then try the 18K acid and so forth. If the line disappeared in front of your eyes while testing the 10K acid, this means your item is not gold or you can usually say its junk. If the item you are testing held to 10K and then held to 14K and then disappeared at 18K, this would mean your item is 14K, but not 18 karat. Once you get the hang of testing the gold it will come natural to you. When you use these acids, do not breathe in the fumes and if you get the acids on your skin, flush it with water immediately. Acids are acids and are dangerous if misused.

You can test gold with nitric acid also. Here you would have to scratch the item and put the acid onto the item. If its gold it will stay bright and shiny. If its junk, it will turn black. When using nitric acid, be very careful. If you get it on your skin, wash it off fast. This acid is also dangerous if misused too.

Silver acid can tell if your item is silver or not. The silver acid is put right onto the silver piece being tested. If the item being tested turns blood red it is silver. If it has a yellowish/reddish tint to it, the item is junk. Its easy to tell with this acid. And of course be careful using it.

There is an electronic gold testing device out on the market now that will tell you what karat gold you have. This gold testing device comes with a set of instructions and costs about $200.00 or so.

There is also a basic non acid gold and silver test kit out too. You have no need to worry about the acids while using this kit. It can tell you if the item is gold or junk. It can also tell you if the item is silver of junk. It cannot tell you what karat the gold item is. This gold and silver test kit sells for around $30.00.

Now that you know that your jewelry is gold and not junk, you may like to sell your jewelry and get some money for it. To be smart about it before you go walking into a store to sell your gold, you should weigh it. Weighing your gold will give you an idea of how much you can get for the gold in scrap. Most places pay for scrap gold with whatever the gold market is doing for that particular day.

Weighing gold is either in pennyweights or in grams. There is 20 pennyweights to an ounce of gold. There is 31.5 grams to an ounce of gold. There are 12 ounces to a pound of gold. Whether you weigh in pennyweights or grams using the calculations will give you a ball park figure on how much you should get back in paper money.

A good scale is worth its weight in gold. If you are using a triple beam scale it will give you a really good accurate weight measurement for your gold. There are some other inexpensive scales out on the market that will give you your ball park figure of how much your gold weighs too. Some of these scales weigh in pennyweights only, some weigh in both pennyweights and grams.

Weighing your gold is very important to see how much you have!

To calculate the gold is easy. To calculate how much the buyer will pay you is easy too if you know the percentage he is buying at.

To calculate:

24 karat gold is 100% gold.
Market gold price is what gold is trading for in the precious metals market of the day.
Example:
For 18K; market gold price x .75 = amount of 18K gold in an ounce.

For 14K; market gold price x .585 = amount of 14K gold in an ounce.
For 10K; market gold price x .417 = amount of 10K gold in an ounce.

Now for the actual price you are going to get for your gold is another story. No one pays 100% for your gold. You have to realize the person you are selling your gold to has to make a profit when they sell their gold to a refinery or another dealer. If you take your gold into a pawn shop you are going to get hardly nothing for your gold. Pawn shops usually pay between 20% to maybe 40% for your gold. Jewelry stores on the other hand will give you a higher price. Jewelry stores will pay between 65% to maybe 85% for your scrap gold. Coin stores may pay 65% to 75% for the gold. If you bring in 4 pieces of gold to a jewelry store, you can probably expect to receive 65% of scrap gold. If you saved up your gold and brought in 30 pieces of gold into the jewelry store, you should be able to get your 85% or maybe even 89% for your scrap gold. You may even be able to work a deal out with the owner of the jewelry store to give you a little more money for the rings that have diamonds or other stones in them.

Now to calculate the gold to find out how much you will actually get back when you scrap your gold.

Let's say you are going to scrap out an ounce of 14K gold at 80% to the dealer. Let's say market price is $500.00 per ounce.
Market gold price x .585 x 80% = total price of the gold you should expect to get back. Example below:
$500.00 x .585 x 80% = $234.00 an ounce of 14K gold you should expect to get back.

Below is an example to calculate your ounce figure of 14K gold to pennyweights (DWT.) or grams. You should know how much you will get for a pennyweight or a gram of gold. This is easy too.

Ounce of 14K gold divided by either the pennyweight or the gram.
$234.00 divided by 20 (pennyweights) = $11.70 per pennyweight.
$234.00 divided by 31.5 (grams) = $7.43 per gram.
This first calculation is what a jewelry store may pay you.

Let's say you bring in an ounce of 14K gold to a pawn shop at 35%. $500.00 x .585 x 35% = $102.38 an ounce is what you can expect from the pawn shop dealer.

Ounce of 14K gold divided by either the pennyweight or the gram.
$102.38 divided by 20 (pennyweights) = $5.12 per pennyweight.
$102.38 divided by 31.5 (grams) = $3.25 per gram.
This second calculation would be what to expect from a pawn shop.

You loose $131.62 per ounce of gold if you brought your gold into a pawn shop. The smart thing to do is call around a few places and ask how much do they pay percentage wise for scrap gold. Tell them you are selling 14K gold and you can get a good calculation from there. Try to sell your gold to the top scrap gold buyer. If you have more 18K or 10K get the prices for these two karats also.

To find the going price of gold, pick up any newspaper and in the business section of the paper you will find the gold market price of gold that day. The market price does fluctuate like the stock market, but you will have an idea of what gold is trading for. You can also find the market price for silver in the newspaper too.

If your selling gold that particular day, you can call any jewelry store or coin shop to get the market price for gold that day.

Now, there is another way of selling gold. That is selling the gold straight to the gold refiners. These companies pay the most. The only problem is, of course, they buy large quantities. Some companies will pay you 98% to 99% for your scrap gold, but you have to sell them 10 pounds of gold or more. That is some serious beach hunting to get 10 pounds of gold accumulated. Also, as a reminder, the refineries pay you in a company check from the refinery and not in cash.

An easy way to sell your gold you found is by selling them to co-workers or friends. If you found a nice 14K gold man's ring and you see it advertised in the local paper for about $150.00. You can usually sell it for at least half of that. People will buy jewelry if they know their getting a good deal on it.

Diamond rings are hard to sell unless you sell them to friends or friends of friends. Same thing, if you see a diamond ring in the store for $800.00 similar to the one you just found, you can probably sell it for $300.00 to $400.00. If you scraped that same ring and it was 14K gold you would get scrap gold price for it. Most dealers won't even look at buying a diamond ring from you unless it's one karat diamond or larger. Quarter karats, half karats and total weight karat diamond rings are common and don't bring in hardly any profit. Unless you sell these types of rings to friends.

If you can and enjoy keeping the rings for show and tell, this is the best pleasure of the treasure hunt. Finding rings and them showing them off is a great reward. It is really fun to see someone's gold ring collection and they may have hundreds of rings to show you. It's what treasure hunting is all about.

A Rolex watch found in the water in south Florida.

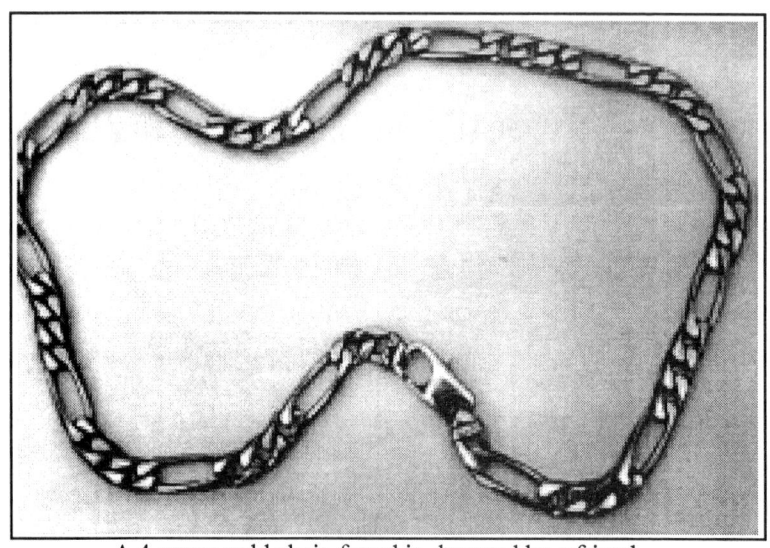

A 4 ounce gold chain found in dry sand by a friend.

DRY SAND BEACH HUNTING TIPS

Beach hunting takes a little practice to understand where to go on the dry sandy beach. Most beaches are so wide and long that it is almost like pot luck to find an area to dig targets constantly. In this chapter there will be some tips on where to hunt and what to look for while searching the dry sand beach.

Dry sand is very popular to most metal detecting people. It is also easy to dig in the sand. All one needs to do is walk out onto the sand, turn their metal detector on and go. One winds up walking up and down the beach swinging the coil back and forth looking to uncover some treasures. Sounds easy enough.

Well, if you had a better idea of how to read the beach you are about to metal detect, you will be able to find the hot spots that will pay off for you is better than guessing. It's pretty easy for the dry sand hunters. If you decide to detect in the early morning or in the evening after everyone goes home, you need to know where to detect at. The smartest thing to do is go over to the beach right in the mid part of the day and see where all the beach people are sunbathing on the beach. This is one of the best ways to increase your treasure finds.

Public beaches are the most profitable beaches to metal detect at. These beaches are packed with locals and tourists from all over the world. Any coastal beach area is very active in the season, whether its Florida or New Jersey. When it's the season, the tourists and sunbathers are there to enjoy the beach.

Most sunbathers try to get as close to the water as possible. They usually set their towels 10' to 15' above the high tide line. This way they don't have to go that far to jump into the water when they are hot and need to cool off. Also, parents are at this area to keep a watch on their children to make sure their safe. For the detectorist, walking along this section of the beach can be more profitable in your finds.

Keep your eyes open for where people have put their towels down in the sand. These spots are easy to spot. Most people shove drink cups or cans into the sand around their towels. Smokers wind up using the sand as one big ash tray with the butts sticking up out of the sand. You can normally see the towel imprints on the sand too. This is also a good area to detect because people may have lost stuff off their towels or blankets. Search the outer edges where you may think the towels were and also search the areas where the towels or blankets were lying. Sometimes when people gather up their belongings, they drop things into the sand right where the towels sat.

Towels are a very useful item at the beach. Most people lay on them at the beach and most people dry themselves off with the towels. Here is another story I have seen over and over again. People put the towels on the sand to lay on. They may want to go into the water to cool off and have some fun. They take off their rings and other jewelry, car keys, wallet and coins from their pocket and either put it in their shoes or wrap the corner of the towel. They head out into the water to have fun. Later they come back out of the water and first thing they grab is their towel to dry off. Now since there is sand all over it they have to flip the towel to get the sand off. AND, guess what, the things they put in the corner of their towel is somewhere scattered all over the beach in the sand. My, my how did that happen they think. And what am I going to do now, as they panic to retrieve their things they just threw into the sand. It's a typical problem with using the towel for a dual purpose to sit on and then to dry off. You guessed it, a treasure hunters dream.

Some beaches rent out lounge chairs and umbrellas to the sun worshipers. This is also a good area to detect around. Some rental chairs are none removable and are lined up in a row. This makes it easy to detect the line and if it's a busy day, your finds may be plentiful. The beach shack that rents this type of equipment is also a good area to detect around, due to, its the place where the money is exchanged. People may drop their change into the sand there.

If the beach you are visiting has restrooms or a concession stand, this is very good for beach hunting. The hundreds of trips back and forth to either the restrooms or the snack bar for the people can cause their coins and jewelry to get lost in the sand. A restaurant or hotel that has a patio bar is excellent. People wind up running back and forth to the patio bar for soft drinks or alcoholic beverages will also wind up loosing some things. A heavy traveled path in the sand is easy to spot. Search all along these beach walkways in the sand to recover many treasures.

Other areas to metal detect on the beach are volley ball courts, picnic areas, park benches, underneath boardwalks and piers. All these areas are good spots to swing your metal detector. Some piers have soda machines on them. Look directly under the machines under the pier. You can find lots of quarters this way.

The showers are also a good place to swing the metal detector. Last week a treasure hunting picked up a 14K gold chain with a medallion on it right next to the showers. He really didn't need his detector to find it. The chain was laying right there in plain sight. But if he wasn't up there to detect around the showers, he would have not find it.

Beach parking meters are good to search around too. Lots of quarters are found around the meters. The sand seems to swallow them up as soon as the quarters hit the sand.

Some beaches have concrete walls to keep the sand from drifting into the streets. People will sit on the wall either facing the ocean or the street. Change gets lost here pretty well from the pockets of pants.

The beach in the evening makes a romantic night for couples. Here you can find just about anything in the sand that may have been left behind. Young adults hang out at the beach at night having fun. At night it is very hard to find anything if it drops into the sand. Usually the item that gets dropped in the sand at night becomes the treasure hunters find the next day.

An excellent time to metal detect the beach is right after a rain storm comes in off the ocean. It's kind of funny because all the people at the beach usually have their bathing suits on. But when that rain starts, they grab everything and head for their cars hurrying fast so they don't get wet. I laugh at this all the time, when I see the rain storms coming in. It is very good to detect because the people are grabbing their belongings so quickly, that they drop stuff into the sand and don't think about it because they are getting wet from the rain. Now, that really takes the cake being wet from the ocean and getting wet from the rain! Makes me laugh.

If you decide to metal detect up behind any of the hotels that are up and down the coastlines, your possibilities of finding lost items are slim. This is due to not having the thousands of people on the beach all the time. Still, a good find from behind one of these hotels may be worth it. Coins may be scarce, but a nice piece of jewelry may help that beach hunters spirit.

You never know what you will dig up out of the dry sand on any given day. Always keep your eyes on the ground while swinging your coil. Here is where eyeballing comes into effect while detecting. As you scan the sand back and forth, your eyes should be looking down at the coil. This way you might find some green paper money sticking out of the sand. You can also eyeball a piece of jewelry this way too.

Always pick up the trash and put it into your trash side of your coin/trash apron. I pick up all the cigarette packages I see and put them into my trash pouch. I'm glad I do. I picked up this Marlboro hard pack one day and inside of the cigarette pack was two 14K gold rings and $45.00 in bills stuffed in the pack too. You never know what people stick in the cigarette packs. A burger bag may have some loose change inside it also. Look for unusual things on the beach while swinging the coil. I found all types of odd ball treasures three or four feet away from where I have been detecting just because my eyes are always wandering around on the sand.

In sand it is very easy to kick some extra sand into a hole and then move on to your next target. Take along your trash you dig up too.

WET SAND BEACH HUNTING

Wet sand beach hunting can either be terrific or terrible. The wet sand is the sand that is wet right down by the waters' edge. The tides can change the area of the wet sand from such a wide area to detect to a very short section of wet sand.

In the summertime, wet sand hunting is very difficult because there are not many targets in the sand. The wintertime is more likely for the wet sand to produce good finds and many of them. The winter brings in the winter storms and the ocean is ferocious most of the time. With the waves and wind pounding the coastline, the sand starts to cut away from the beach. This produces the targets to be uncovered and easier to reach with a metal detector.

Summer may bring some storms to cut the beach or the wind may blow a little harder than usual from a good direction to cut any of the beaches. But most of the time metal detecting in the wet sand in the summer is usually a waste of time. Unless you do not mind walking many of miles in the wet sand to dig a target or two.

What does make a beach cut in the summer is if there is a hurricane that either skirts along the coast line or comes into shore at any time. This does tear up the beach and erodes the beach several feet down. Some beaches along the Florida coast after a tropical storm or hurricane had a very steep drop off to get down onto the beach. I have been on Ft. Lauderdale beach after Hurricane David in 1979 and had to jump down ten feet to get onto the beach. This much sand removed from any beach produces hundreds and hundreds of coins and jewelry in a short period of time.

This is why winter storms are good. The storm will rip apart the beach and erode it down to a layer of sand that may produce coins and jewelry every swing of the metal detector. The winter storms will keep the beach cut most of the season. If the beach cuts in a few days and then fills back in, the next week may bring in more waves and more cuts on the beach.

Shown above is a small beach cut at Pompano Beach.

Some hunters can walk right out onto the beach and look up and down the beach and be able to tell if the wet sand will produce. Here are some tips for you to look for to help you do the same. A good start is if you walk out onto the wet sand and your feet sink up to your ankles. This means the sand is too soft and all the targets you want to detect are going to be unreachable with your metal detector. That is probably the number one clue for you not to hunt the wet sand. If this happens your better off metal detecting in the dry sand. You will find more treasures there.

Another tip is to see if the wet sand may produce, is by looking up and down the beach in the wet sand. What you are looking for are any scallops or dips along the coastline. This may take you a few times out to realize what you are looking for when you are staring up and down the beach. Big scallops and dips are very easy to spot. It's the shallow scallops and dips that are hard to recognize. A scallop or dip is an area in the wet sand that dips down a little lower in the sand. This is where the sand is removed maybe an extra few inches up to several feet off the coastline. These areas can produce handfuls of coins and jewelry if the conditions are right.

The scalloped areas in this photo are where the wet sand meets the dry sand.

When you start to recognize these scallops and dips, you will start to find more treasures in the wet sand. Think of it this way. The upper edges of the scallops are peaks and the scallops are valleys. You want to metal detect in the valley rather than on a peak. The upper edges of the scallops are the softer sand. At this point, this softer sand is where you will find the lighter things, like pulltabs and other aluminum junk. The valley or scallops are where the heavier items will settle, like coins and jewelry. This is the gold mine you are looking for.

Now the easiest tip of all, are the beach cuts. Beach cuts is like a step off from the dry sand onto the wet sand. It is a natural 90 degree drop off onto the wet sand. Some cuts are only a few inches deep. Some cuts are a few feet deep and some other cuts can be several feet deep. At this point the beach is washed away from the wall of the cut to the ocean.

Working a cut like this will produce lots of coins and jewelry. Sometimes if the cut is large, you can be swinging your detector and eyeballing the coins right on the surface. With the beach cut like that, you may swing your detector coil and receive several beeps all in one pass and everything you dig up are coins and an occasional piece of jewelry.

When working any cuts or scallops the tides are a big factor in your successful hunts. If you decide to metal detect at high tide, the beach is not very wide and your finds are not very good. Check the tides with the newspaper or the Weather Channel for the beach you are going to detect at. Low tide is the best tide to hunt. To metal detect at low tide you may want to get to the beach two to three hours before low tide and chase the waves back into the ocean. This gives you more time to hunt and as the ocean is receding, it is removing more sand off the beaches. When the tide switches from low tide and starts coming back up to high tide, the ocean is then bringing some sand back up onto the beaches. Your finds at the low tide hunting should be very profitable.

If the beaches are cut and you are heading to the Treasure Coast to metal detect the 1715 beaches looking for treasure coins. You will want to know this tip. You will want to show up at the treasure beaches about a half hour before high tide. These beaches here you want to metal detect from high tide and chase the waves back into the ocean towards low tide. If you wait until low tide to hunt these beaches, you will have missed your chance. The locals will have been detecting these beaches ahead of you. The treasure beaches are probably the only beach hunting you want to start during high tide.

Any of the rest of the beaches along the coast, you will want to metal detect at a couple of hours before low tide.

In winter type conditions, when the ocean is ferocious and the waves are ripping apart the coastline you will want to be very careful at the waters' edge. Here, both large and small pieces of wood can come ashore and hit you while you are swinging your detector. Try not to stop a piece of wood floating at you with your foot. You may break your foot or get a bad bruise from the force of the wave action.

When the waves are strong and bring water high up on the beaches, keep your eyeballs on the ground. You may see some green paper money come floating out of the sea. You have to be quick because as fast as the money comes out of the sea. It will disappear back into the sea with the waves just as quick. You can also spot coins and rings tumbling in the surf line too if you pay attention. When a ring gets tossed up out of the ocean move quickly and try and catch it in your scoop or it may be lost until next time.

Wet sand is really fun when the conditions are right and the surf is not pounding on the coast. When it is right you will dig hundreds of scoopfuls of sand and find hundreds of coins and several pieces of jewelry. Always remember to cover your scoop holes after digging out the target so no one will trip in it. It is good practice to cover your holes wherever you are metal detecting. Good luck.

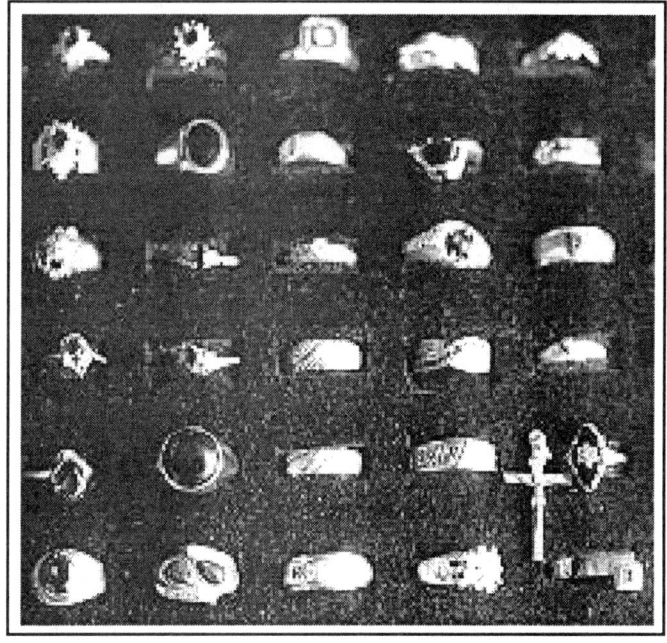

Rings found both in the wet sand and in the ocean.

Just a reminder not to leave your valuables in visible site in your car.

SHALLOW WATER TREASURE HUNTING!

Beach hunting all year long is fun. Wet sand hunting in the winter is exciting. Yet another fun time is shallow water treasure hunting. In the summer months this can be really fun and it is very refreshing. After a long hot summer day of working, it sure is a pleasure to go to the beach with the detector and scoop and go in the water.

On summer mornings there is hardly any wind blowing in south Florida. This means there are no waves and the ocean is like a sheet of glass and crystal clear. When you walk out into the ocean up to your neck, you can see your feet. This makes shallow water hunting enjoyable. And to top it off, the water temperature is usually in the 80's. A shallow water hunter can swing their detector all day long and be very comfortable.

When the ocean is flat in the mornings the water hunter can search a pattern in the water with no trouble. Seeing where to put your scoop in the sand is a plus. Also when you miss your target or it falls out of your scoop you can see it to recover it again. I once had a gold charm fall through my scoop bucket several times before I got to see it on the sand. Once I saw it laying there I just dove under the water and picked it up. Crystal clear water is sure a nice way to water hunt.

In the afternoon along the Florida's coast, the winds usually start to pick up and the ocean becomes choppy. This makes water hunting a little more difficult. You have to bop around with the waves and pay more attention to recovering your targets. Still this type of hunting is fine too. You can usually see the bottom pretty well, so you can dig your targets up.

Some days the wind is really blowing. This makes water hunting almost impossible to hunt. When the waves are rolling in and are a couple of feet high this makes it a real challenge to detect. Here, you will be either ducking under the waves as they roll by or trying to jump over them. For sure, you can water hunt in these condition, but sometimes it is really tricky. Besides jumping over the waves you have to plant your scoop in the sand and retrieve your targets without getting pushed away from the hole you are trying to dig. Sometimes a wave will go by and the scoopful of sand you just dug up is washed out of your bucket and the item mysteriously disappears too. Now you have to try and find the missing target because in the back of your mind you know it can be a gold ring. This type of hunting takes patience and practice to accomplish, but it can be done.

Another thing you must learn about shallow water hunting in the ocean is to follow the tides. If the ocean is rough, you won't be able to get out deep enough to detect if the tide is high. Here is where you would want to hunt at low tide.

The religious medallion was found in shallow water at low tide.

When the ocean is flat, you can go out farther into the ocean at low tide and recover the targets that are on the downside of the sand bar. At high tide you will be either hunting right on the sand bar or just in front of the sand bar. If the ocean is flat either tide is good to hunt. Still, hunting low tide seems to be nicer because you are hunting where the people were swimming earlier. At high tide the bathers can only go out so deep before it is over their heads. At low tide your detecting in waist deep water where at high tide it was neck deep water. This is an advantage to the shallow water hunter.

In the summer, you are looking for freshly lost jewelry. The swimmers are making their deposits of loosing their coins and jewelry on the sand bars. The sand bars are everywhere in the summer. This is one reason you are looking for the freshly lost treasure. Sand really doesn't shift around too much in the summer like it does in the winter. Some summer currents will move sand and open up some pockets, but it happens occasionally. You need a combination of current, wind and waves to shift the sand around.

Beach people go to the beach to lay out on their towels and then go jump in the water to cool off and have fun. One thing most bathers do is put on their suntan lotions to protect their skin from the sun. Well, a little suntan lotion and some water makes their rings slide off their fingers very easily in the water. This is a big plus for the water hunters. This is one reason it is very good for water hunting.

Other reasons why water hunting in the ocean is becoming very popular is because there is less trash in the ocean. Let me make that more clearer. It is not less trash, it is that the trash like aluminum pulltabs and other junk tend to shift in close to the beach. This junk usually winds up right at that first drop off trough as you step into the ocean. Junk is light and it gathers up with the tiny light shells that are right at the sand where the first drop off begins. A few feet out away from the drop off it starts to become better detecting. Ocean currents will shift the lighter junk in towards the beach leaving the coins and jewelry out further on the sand bars.

This is why water hunters enjoy metal detecting in the ocean. The percentages are higher for finding more coins and jewelry. If you are out there digging up a hundred coins in the ocean, you can almost be surprised by only digging up eight or ten pulltabs. You will dig up some other miscellaneous junk in the water. Aluminum cans are a sure bet you will find them every once in awhile. Sun glasses, keys, car toys and maybe a money clip are some of the odd ball stuff that you can dig up also.

Batteries are one of the junk items that can get dug up a few times here and there. The only people who wind up digging up batteries are the people who swing pulse metal detectors. Since the pulses operate in all metal, batteries are detected. Other junk you will find with a pulse detector in the water are fish hooks, nails, bottle cap lids, steel washers, nuts, bolts and after the Forth of July, sparkler wires. If you dig this junk up, remember to bring it with you out of the water and throw it away. You would not want to go in the ocean the next day and dig up the same junk you already dug up.

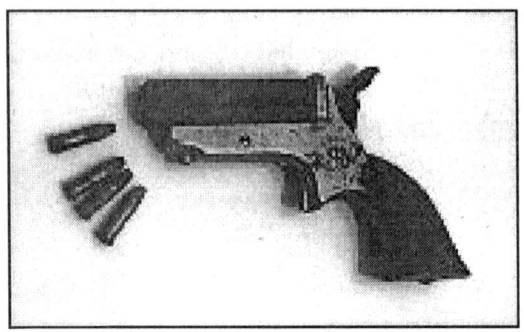

Pistol found by shallow water hunter in the ocean.

If you are metal detecting along a causeway or in bays or lakes these areas really have no current to shift the lighter trash around. So, where the junk is dropped is where you will find it. These areas are also very good to hunt, you may dig a little more trash but that's all right. Rings and jewelry will still fall off easy when mixed with water and suntan lotion.

On the Intracoastal Waterway, side canals and in lakes there are trees extending over the water. Here people will find a good tree and tie a rope to it for a swing. A rope swing is an excellent place to shallow water hunt under because of the items you will find. As the person swings out off the tree on the rope and then lets go, anything that is in their pants pockets will fall out. If they have 30 coins in their pocket, the coins will fall into the water all in the same place. You may dig up several dollars in change with one scoopful if you detect the right area. You can even find rings and chains in the same location. As the people let go of the rope, the rope sometimes snags their rings and slips the rings off their fingers because the persons hands are wet. Doing flips off the rope swing will lead to lost chains. I always enjoy finding a good rope swing to water hunt under.

Recovering your target in the water can be tricky if you don't have the right equipment. This is where a good heavy duty water scoop comes in handy. If you are a water hunter and you invested into a not so good water scoop, you may find yourself on the beach in a short time with a broken scoop. A good reliable water scoop is worth every penny you spend for it. If you spend a hundred dollars for the water scoop and it lasts several years without breaking apart, you will be much more happier. With a good water scoop you can also retrieve your targets quicker and in the end results pay for that water scoop faster with your treasures you find.

A good item for water hunting is a water proof pouch to put your treasures into after you recover them. There are several different pouches out on the market. Some of the pouches are made of a plastic mesh with a velcro closure to secure your treasures. These pouches are made to wear on a belt. Some hunters wear two of these pouches, one for trash and one for their treasures. You really want to put your finds somewhere when you go in the water to detect.

When water hunting in the ocean, you may find a pocket or two. These pockets are formed by the current and waves. It is real easy to find these pockets if you are in the water. Walking in a straight line parallel with the beach in waist deep water, you may come upon a pocket. If you are in waist deep water and you suddenly find yourself in chest deep water and you are still in the same line you started to walk in, you just walked into a pocket. A pocket is a wash out sand area in the ocean. It is similar to a scalloped area on wet sand. The pocket may be only a few inches or a foot or two deep. Detect in the pocket thoroughly. This is where heavier items will settle, such as gold. It may pay off or it may have a few targets in the pocket. You never can tell unless you detect it.

Spotting a pocket from the beach is easy too. The pockets will be the darker blue areas in the ocean. These areas are shown around the lighter blue areas where the sand is more visible. If you walk into the ocean in the darker areas you should be deeper in the water and in a pocket. If you walk into a deeper than usual pocket, search it very carefully. These deeper pockets will reveal more treasure. You may have to have a little patience working a pocket. The deeper pocket may be in neck deep water and harder for you to metal detect in neck deep water. Pockets are excellent areas to detect.

If you venture out to water hunt remember to bring in the trash and discard it in the trash can. It will help you from finding it again. Happy water hunting!

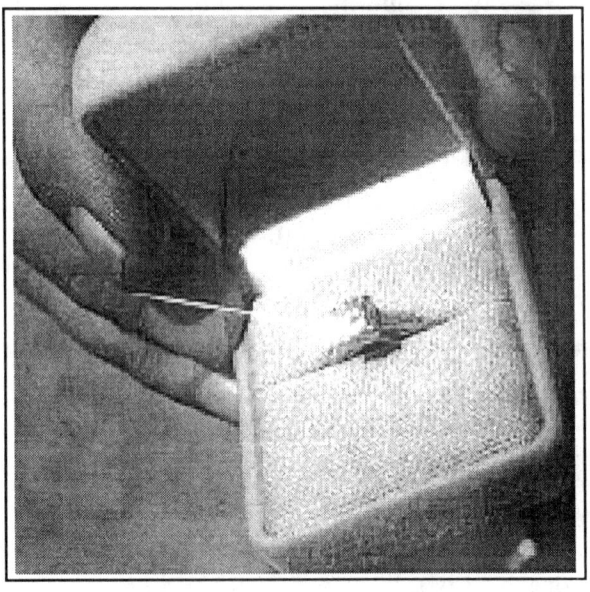

A 1-1/2 carat diamond ring found in the ocean!

BIBLIOGRAPHY

"Hurricane Treasure - 1715 Beach Sites - Locations Revealed" by Kevin Reilly, Gary T. Rowe & Kevin Maranville

"Sunken Treasure On The Florida Reefs - The 1715 Spanish Plate Fleet" by Robert "Frogfoot" Weller

"Shipwrecks In The Americas"   by Robert F. Marx

"Shipwrecks Near Wabasso Beach"   by Weller & Richards

"Florida's Sandy Beaches - An Access Guide"
by University Of West Florida Press/Pensacola

"The Treasure Diver's Guide"   by John S. Potter, Jr.

"Shipwrecks Of Broward County" by James Dean & Steven D. Singer

"Space Coast Dive Directory"   by T.L. Armstrong

"Beachcombing For Treasure"   by Chas. M. Albano

"Treasure Hunting Beach Style"   by Robert Huhnken

"Advanced Water Working Techniques"   by Andy Sabisch

"The New Recovery From Sand & Sea"   by Charles Garrett

"Relics, Water & The Kitchen Sink - A Diver's Handbook To Underwater Archeology"   by Alan R. Rowe

"Florida Atlas & Gazetteer"   by DeLorme Mapping Company

"The Search For Treasure Volume 2"   by Thomas P. Terry

"Shipwrecks Of Florida"   by Steven D. Singer

"What You Need To Know About Your Gold & Silver"   by Oscar T. Branson

"Advanced Shallow Water Treasure Hunting"   by Wallace L. Chandler

"History Under The Sea"   by Mendel Peterson
"Diamonds In The Surf"   by Bob Trevillian & Frank Carter